Little Bible Heroes™
The Little Maid

Written by Victoria Kovacs
Illustrated by Mike Krome

SCHOLASTIC INC.

12 11 10 9 8 7 6 5 4 3 2 1   16 17 18 19 20 21

Printed in the U.S.A.   40

First Scholastic printing, September 2016

A warrior named Naaman is the commander of a big army. One day his army raids Israel and captures a little girl.

The little girl is sad to leave her home, but she makes the best of her new life.

She becomes a servant to Naaman's wife. The girl remembers her home and her God.

Naaman has a terrible sickness. The little servant girl tells him, "Elisha is God's prophet. He can heal you."

Naaman travels to Israel to see Elisha. Elisha says, "Wash in the Jordan River seven times, and you will be healed."

Naaman washes in the river. His sickness is all gone!

Naaman is happy and knows that God has healed him.

Thanks to his little maid, Naaman is healed and learns about God's power.

Read:

Aram had gone on raids and brought back from the land of Israel a young girl who served Naaman's wife.—2 Kings 5:2

Think:

1. Who healed Naaman?
2. The little maid helped Naaman. How can you help people who are sick?

Remember:

"Worship the Lord your God, and He will bless your bread and your water. I will remove illnesses from you."
—Exodus 23:25

PARENT Connection

Read:

The LORD came, stood there, and called as before, "Samuel, Samuel!" Samuel responded, "Speak, for Your servant is listening."
—1 Samuel 3:10

Think:

1. What do you think it was like for little Samuel to grow up in the temple?
2. God speaks to all of us in many ways. What are some ways God speaks to you?

Remember:

"The one who is from God listens to God's words."
—John 8:47

When he grows up, Samuel becomes a great prophet and leader. And he still listens to God.

God calls Samuel again.

"Speak, Lord, your servant is listening," says Samuel.

God answers! This time, Samuel listens and hears an important message from God.

"Here I am. You called me?" Samuel says.

Eli knows that God is calling Samuel. He tells Samuel, "If you are called again, say, 'Speak, Lord. Your servant is listening.'"

Samuel hears someone call his name again. He runs to Eli, but the priest sends him back to bed.

Then Samuel hears someone call him a third time, so he runs and wakes up Eli once more.

One night, when Samuel is sleeping, he hears someone call his name. Samuel runs to Eli.

"Here I am. You called me?" Samuel says.

Eli yawns and shakes his head. "No, I didn't call you. Go back to bed."

Samuel helps the high priest, Eli. Samuel wears a special linen vest that the priests wear. He is a good boy and works hard.

Hannah prays for a baby. God answers her prayers and gives her a baby boy named Samuel.

When Samuel is old enough, he goes to live in God's temple.

Little Bible Heroes™
Samuel

Written by Victoria Kovacs
Illustrated by Mike Krome

SCHOLASTIC INC.

12 11 10 9 8 7 6 5 4 3 2 1   16 17 18 19 20 21

Printed in the U.S.A.   40

First Scholastic printing, September 2016